The
Baby Book

A Dorling Kindersley Book

100 ways to keep your baby smiling

Dorling **DK** Kindersley

LONDON, NEW YORK, SYDNEY, DELHI,
PARIS, MUNICH , and JOHANNESBURG

Senior Managing Art Editor Lynne Brown

Senior Managing Editor Corinne Roberts

Art Editor Glenda Fisher

Project Editor Valerie Kitchenham

DTP Designer Rajen Shah

Production Joanna Bull

Published in the United States by
Dorling Kindersley Publishing, Inc.
95 Madison Avenue, New York,
New York 10016

First American Edition
2 4 6 8 10 9 7 5 3 1

A CIP catalog record for this book is available
from the Library of Congress.

ISBN 0-7894-5950-7

Reproduced by Colourscan, Singapore.
Printed and bound by
South China Printing Co. Ltd

see our complete catalog at
www.dk.com

12-18 months

Ideas 63-100

including: • kitchen fun, and
mealtime tips and treats
• puzzles • farm animals and
animal rhymes • going to the
seaside • doing a workout
• playing ball • going
swimming • bathtime fun

Action rhymes to
enjoy together

Acknowledgments

Introduction

Every day, all over the world, thousands of people experience the thrill of becoming parents to a little bundle of joy who will bring no end of fun into their lives. And for those parents, a primary concern will be to ensure that their baby remains healthy and happy, nurtured by an environment that offers limitless opportunities for development through learning and play.

This is where *The Happy Baby Book* can help. Packed with 100 ideas for keeping your baby amused and occupied, it is designed to inspire parents, grandparents, aunts, uncles, and caregivers alike.

Divided into easy-reference sections according to age suitability, the 100 ideas and activities you'll find in *The Happy Baby Book* will take you and your little one from those first exciting days of babyhood through to the growing independence of early toddlerhood. And, although the ideas are all lighthearted and fun, where appropriate we incorporate information on how they may encourage your baby's development.

We have all sorts of tips for happy times – from entertaining games and silly action rhymes to gentle massage and exciting water play; from fun food and early music-making ideas to rough and tumble and exploring books.

All of the ideas you'll find in *The Happy Baby Book* are based on good common-sense parenting. And, while there may be some you will have already thought of, we hope there will be many times when you'll be glad for the inspiration our 100 ideas provide to try something new to stimulate your baby.

So, why not turn the page and take a look? With its handy mini size, *The Happy Baby Book* provides a source of in-pocket entertainment you can take anywhere and, hopefully, dip into before that bottom lip starts to wobble!

PS If you've forgotten the words of your childhood nursery rhymes, don't worry. Just turn to the back of the book, where we've put together a collection of action-rhyme favorites…

birth - 3 months

THE FIRST THREE MONTHS are an exciting time for you and your baby as you both get to know one another. You'll be thrilled and intrigued as you watch him gradually learn to smile, follow things with his eyes, respond to sounds, and coo with pleasure. At this stage, the key to ensuring your baby's contentment is simply to make him feel loved and secure in his amazing new world. The following 15 ideas will make him feel safe and happy through the reassuring sensations of touch, sight, and sound — what better start in life could you give him?

1

talk to her

Your new baby will love to hear you talk. She'll recognize the rhythms from when she was in the womb, so your voices will be a familiar link with the world she has emerged into.

2

smile at her

Keep smiling! Your baby will look very comical as she starts to copy your various facial expressions.

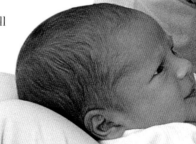

3

sing a lullaby

A baby is born with rhythm. She picks it up from hearing her mother's heartbeat while in the womb and from experiencing the rocking sensation of her walk as she is carried around in her pelvis for nine months. So the sound of a caring voice singing a lilting, rhythmical song is the perfect soother for when she needs calming. If you've forgotten the words of childhood nursery rhymes and lullabies, you can always sing a familiar television program theme tune or any song that your baby hears often. You will find yourself swaying naturally as you sing.

4

keep him cozy

Your baby has no built-in temperature control, so you have to make sure he doesn't get too cold, nor too warm. Lay him on a warm towel to change him.

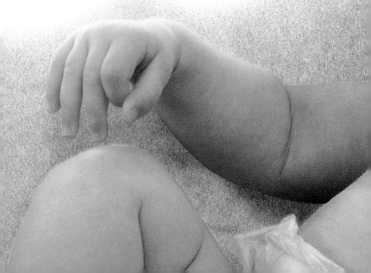

5

make her feel safe

A new baby has new skin, so wrap her in soft, natural materials – she will enjoy their comforting texture. Being wrapped or swaddled makes her feel safe – having spent nine months in a confined space, the big wide world can seem frightening to a tiny baby. Many newborns dislike being naked, so if she seems unsettled at changing times try draping a muslin cloth or diaper over her tummy since this may make her feel happier and less exposed.

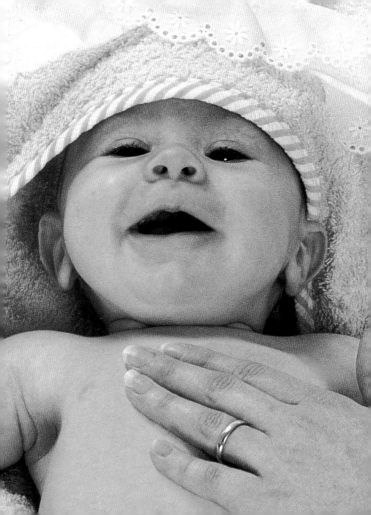

cuddle up close

A baby can be wrapped up as snug as a bug, but there's no substitute for cuddling up to mom. Just lying together for a rest or a feeding is enough for your baby to feel blissfully secure. You can relax, too, and revel in watching him snooze or suckle.

7

give him a mobile

Your newborn can see up to 8–10in (20–25cm) away and by three months he may be able to focus on a mobile. Hang one over his crib and its colorful shapes will delight him. Ensure that the mobile is out of reach if you leave him alone with it.

8

put rings on her wrist...

Bees, butterflies, and bunnies – there are many types of fun
wrist rattles available for your baby to get her hands on. Give
her one to play with and watch her face light up.

9

and bells on her toes!

Help your baby to find her feet by sewing bells on her socks,
but do make sure they're still attached very securely before
you put them on each time. She will love to hear them tinkle.

10

let teddy take over...

...so you can have a break from providing the entertainment. Nothing beats the timeless child appeal of a big soft teddy bear – babies find their faces fascinating. Make sure any cuddly toy you give your child complies with all current safety standards.

11

bring in
big brother

Babies find children intriguing, so let an older brother
or sister (or a friendly tame toddler!) try entertaining for
awhile. But never leave an older child alone with a baby.

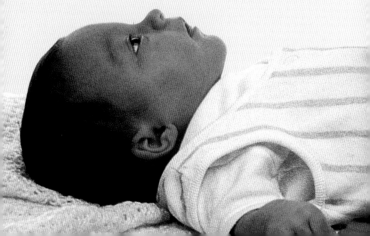

Get out and about with...

12

...a carrier

This is a nifty solution for transporting your baby, both in and out of the car. Some designs fit onto accompanying baby carriage/stroller frames, too, for added versatility.

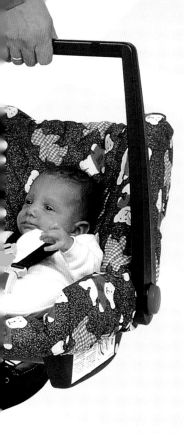

13

...a baby carriage

Just getting fresh air and seeing a friend will change the mood of a fractious day. Get out for a walk with the baby carriage or stroller – prop up your baby so she can look around.

14

...a sling

A sling is a very handy means of transport, since it offers your baby comforting body contact and allows you to carry her while leaving your hands free.

re

laaaax

3 - 6 months

DURING THESE MONTHS you'll notice your baby becoming more sociable as she burbles and chuckles and takes greater notice of people around her. She'll study things closely as her focusing improves, and everything she touches will end up in her mouth as she explores texture and taste. This is a fun time as she gains the strength to roll from her back to her front and push herself up. The next 19 ideas will all encourage her to learn about her body and what it can do – from playing with her toes to splashing in water, enjoying new tastes to bopping in a baby jumper.

blow a raspberry!

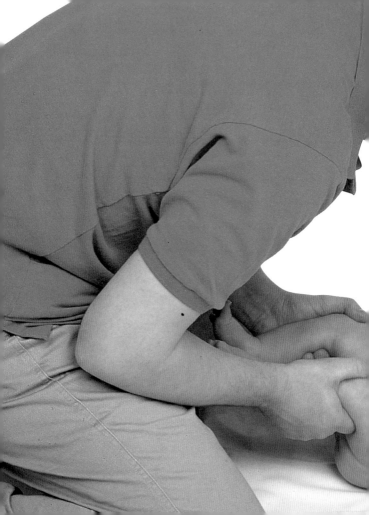

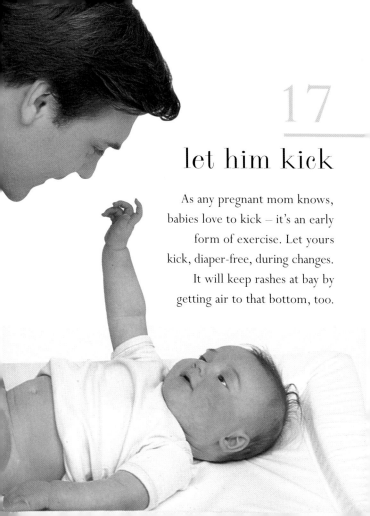

let him kick

As any pregnant mom knows,
babies love to kick – it's an early
form of exercise. Let yours
kick, diaper-free, during changes.
It will keep rashes at bay by
getting air to that bottom, too.

18

"massage me!"

Nothing is more soothing than a gentle all-over massage – it's the natural way to establish a bond with your baby through touch. First, make sure the room is warm and your baby is content, then lay him on a thick towel. Working downward from shoulders to feet, lightly move your hands over his body, using a little baby oil to soften his skin. Talk or sing to him as you go, or play relaxing music in the background.

19

"tickle
me!"

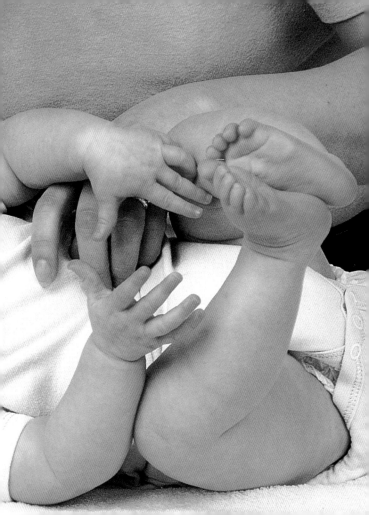

20

play with her fingers...

Your baby will soon begin to explore her own hands and fingers and you can join in with these discoveries by singing hand-action rhymes with her. A fun rhyme to sing is *One, two, three, four, five / Once I caught a fish alive*...

21

play with her toes...

Her toes are a source of wriggly fascination for your baby. By gently touching each toe in turn, you can stimulate her range of sensations – and guarantee getting a giggle! Try playing *This little pig went to market* while she is lying down having her diaper changed or when she is snuggled up close on your knee.

22

...then let her try!

Gotcha! Once your baby knows they're there, her hands and toes will become her favorite playthings. Give her the freedom to get to know her own body — it will contribute to her developing sense of self-awareness. By grabbing her toes, she is experimenting with hand-eye coordination and starting to understand perspective.

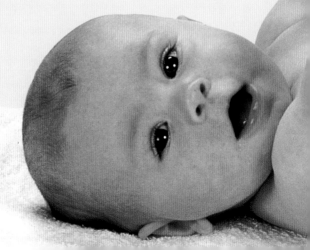

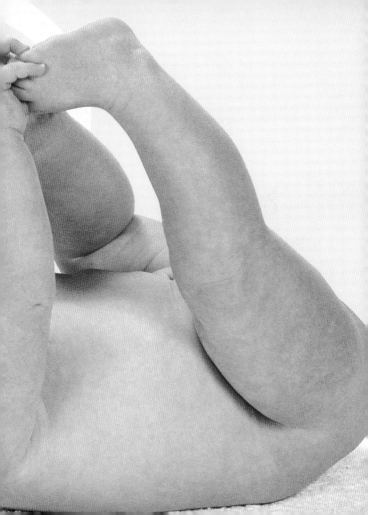

Show him the world...

23 ...from a ringside seat

Once your baby can hold his head up – maybe from as early
as six weeks – you can pop him in a baby chair. This will
make him feel more involved in what's going on. Never put
the chair on a table or leave him unattended while he's in it.

24 ...in a mirror

Let him look in a mirror, then talk to him about the little boy
he can see there. He will be intrigued by the puzzled face that
is peering back at him.

25 ...from up high and all around

With a baby jumper, your baby can spin himself around and
bop up and down. He will be thrilled by the freedom it offers
him to see the world from an upright position.

26

give him
some space

As your baby approaches six months, he may be able to sit propped up by cushions. Encourage him to try – you'll find he loves the sense of freedom it gives him. Put his favorite toys in front of him, sit back, and give him some space to enjoy playing by himself. It's important that he learns to enjoy periods of quieter, more introspective play so that you can intersperse these with more energetic forms of activity as he gets older. This way he'll learn to enjoy his own company as well as that of others.

Make mealtimes scrummy

27

...puréeing

Simply push cooked fruit or vegetables through a sieve.

28

...steaming

This maintains nutrients – most vegetables steam well.

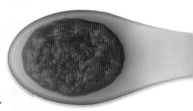

29

...poaching

To poach, cook fruit and vegetables in a little water.

and textures yummy by...

30

...mashing

Bananas mash beautifully,
but so do juicy mangoes.

31

...blending

Be daring – blend flavors,
such as apple and pear.

32

...combining

Combine textures, such as
baby rice with zucchini.

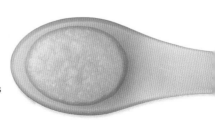

As soon as your baby can grab and hold an object, she'll enjoy some simple bathtime toys. Bright yellow ducks are the old favorite, especially if they come in families. She can play with one, while the others bob about around her.

go quackers!

34

have a happy
water baby

Your baby may love her bath, but hair-washing is often another matter entirely. Many babies dislike water and bubbles running into their eyes, so minimize bathtime tears by gently sponging water onto her head rather than allowing it to trickle down onto her face. Or you could buy a shampoo guard – this is designed to shield the eyes from soapy dribbles.

6-12 months

AT THIS STAGE in his development, your little
one goes from barely being able to sit up to
taking his first few faltering steps. By his first
birthday you'll wonder where your little baby has
gone! This is a time of rapid progress as your
child's hearing, coordination, and spatial
awareness become increasingly sophisticated and
his growing strength and balance allow him to
learn to sit alone, crawl, and pull himself up to
cruise around the furniture. Now it is variety
that's the key to keeping your child happy and
stimulated – turn the page for more clever ideas
that are guaranteed to keep him smiling…

35

send in a granny

Any granny (or grandpa!) will do the trick – they are all past masters in the art of baby entertainment and know no end of rhymes, games, and pacifying techniques that are guaranteed to work. What they can offer your baby is different from what you can offer, and that's the secret of their success – after all, variety is the spice of life, even when you're six months old.

help him sleep easy

An older baby doesn't automatically doze off in your arms after a feeding, so you can no longer expect to put him in his crib already asleep. To ensure happy bedtimes, he needs to get used to going to bed while he's awake and learn to get off to sleep alone without getting anxious. You can help by making his crib an interesting place to be with toys and a mobile (out of reach when he's alone with it). This will help when he wakes in the morning, too, since he may play for awhile before calling you.

"go, baby, go!"

Once your baby is mobile, there's no stopping her, so baby-proof your home and create a safe area where she will be able to explore freely. She needs watching, but you'll be more relaxed if you reduce the hazards. If you want to keep her "captive" for awhile, use a mesh-sided playpen.

give him something safe to...

...throw

...chew

...stack

play
peek-a-

40

give him a box!

It's an old joke among parents, but babies
often do seem to prefer the box to the gift
inside it. So, forget the new toy, just give
your baby an empty box (without
staples or sharp edges) and
he'll be happy.

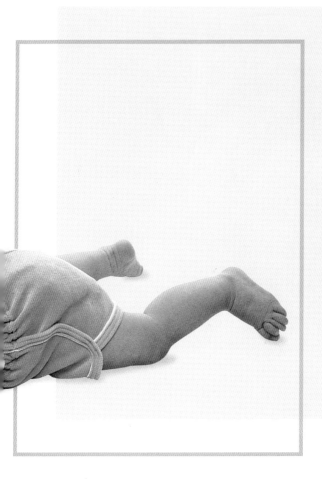

sing...

Row, row, row
your boat,

gently down the
stream,

merrily, merrily,
merrily, merrily,

life is but a
dream.

play in the sand

Sifting, molding, and mixing sand will keep your baby busy. Always fit a lid on the pit, so the sand stays clean.

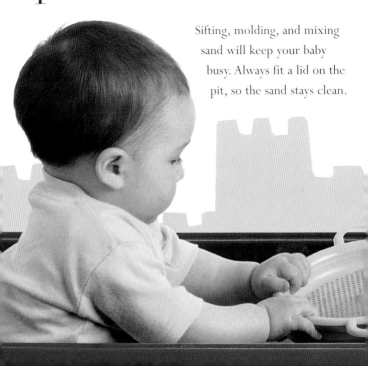

Go into the
garden and...

43

dig in a
flowerpot

44

roll on
the grass

45

listen for birds

46

smell the flowers...

Take your baby into the garden or to the park to show him the flowers. Talk to him about their bright colors and let him smell them and handle their petals. He'll be intrigued by their fragrance and velvety texture. Although they might look good enough to eat, make sure none ends up in his mouth.

47

... and feel the leaves

Pick leaves for him to handle and scrunch up, and tickle his nose with blades of grass. Early experiences like this are important as a means of introducing him to nature and the world around him.

Rock 'n' roll

48

let him jingle
some bells...

50

shake some
maracas...

49

strike a
xylophone...

51

bang a toy
drum or...

52

... a saucepan!

Give her a pan to bash with a wooden spoon. She'll love to hear the satisfying "dong."

53

click spoons

She can click wooden spoons together or "play" the fridge door. You have been warned!

54

make a shaker

Take a small plastic bottle and pour in some dry rice. Ensure the top is securely tightened.

55

listen to notes

Fill empty plastic bottles with varying levels of water. Blow over the top of each. Listen…

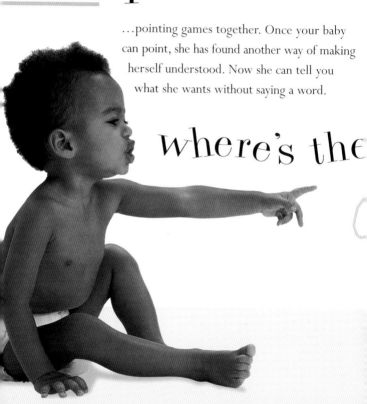

56 play...

...pointing games together. Once your baby can point, she has found another way of making herself understood. Now she can tell you what she wants without saying a word.

where's the

give grandpa
a call

58

give him a cookie

Get gums chewing and new teeth nibbling with healthy snacks. If his tummy is rumbling, finger foods will fill the gap. Try a stick of cheese or carrot, chopped seedless grapes or slices of banana. The occasional plain cookie is good, too. Always watch while he eats in case anything goes down the wrong way.

59

...or let him get stuck in!

60

"give her a hug"

Make your baby happy by booking up a busy social life with little friends. Ensure success by keeping visits to playmates short but sweet, so there's no time for tears.

61

use up
some
energy

There's nothing more exhilarating than the
sensation of being whisked through the air.
Your baby will thrill to some safe, controlled
rough and tumble – but don't overdo it.

62

enjoy books

A book is amazing. It opens and closes, has colorful pictures and words that make stories, and, if it's a board book, your baby can chew it and drop it, and it will still be fun to look at.

12 - 18 months

THIS IS THE TIME of walking and talking and you'll find your child goes up a gear and wants to be into everything. As well as experimenting with his first real steps and first real words, he will be fascinated by books and scribbling and will enjoy feeding himself at mealtimes. And, as his balance and confidence grow, he'll become more surefooted and will soon be charging about, busying himself in a world of pretend play, copying your behavior and conversational chit-chat. To prevent boredom, let him enjoy his growing independence – the following ideas offer some useful ways of keeping him interested and amused.

63

buy him a spare snuggle bunny

If your baby has formed an attachment with one particular toy, the chances are he'll love it so hard that it will end up looking nothing like the teddy or baa-lamb it once was. A clever tip is to buy a spare – an identical "snuggle bunny" or "cuddly" that you can substitute once the original has seen better days or interchange with the other to make both last longer.

64 ...a peg game

Fitting the right shape in the right hole can be quite difficult, so your child will need your help to begin with.

65 ...a giant jigsaw

Go for specially designed big-piece jigsaw puzzles. They will help to develop hand-eye coordination.

66 ...a shape-sorter

This toy requires your child to put 3-D shapes through their corresponding window and encourages shape-matching skills.

67 ...pairing cards

A card game involving matching up identical images of animals, for example, has a simple appeal. Always give lots of praise.

Set him a puzzle

challenge with...

Tiny hands can...

68 roll pastry

69 decorate cookies

70 stack saucepans

71 help lay place mats

72 put fruit in the bowl

73 help unpack shopping

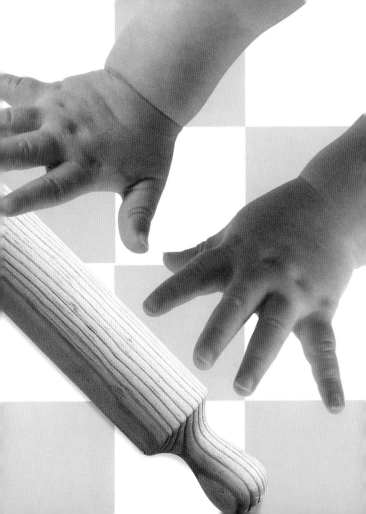

make mealtimes

Bring your baby to the table and make eating a sociable affair.
Put the highchair away and use a booster seat for family
meals. Give him his own cutlery
and introduce new tastes.

lots of fun...

...with fabulous fish

Babies can be fickle eaters, so it pays to be inventive when introducing new tastes. If you find it hard to tempt your child at mealtimes, try experimenting with the way in which you present her food. Why not be inspired by this fishy dish (flaked fish spooned inside a yellow-pepper outline) to make

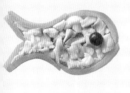

make a tasty

all sorts of appetizing treats to tempt your child? Think about how you might use nutritious staples, such as fruit, vegetables, bread and pasta to create fun food animals or comical faces on her plate. She'll probably enjoy eating her peas and carrots if she thinks she's eating a scary monster's eyes and nose!

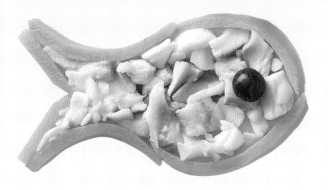

ocean dish

...and busy bees

Bees, butterflies, beetles, and spiders – there are all sorts of nice and nasty things you can serve up as dessert! Take ice cream, gelatin, or blancmange, and get creative...

make creepy

take some ice cream...

Take a scoop of ice cream and place in a dish.
Decorate with chocolate-chip eyes, licorice legs, or wafer
wings – whatever you fancy to create your creepy-crawly.

wobbly gelatin...

Make up gelatin according to packet instructions. Pour into
small individual molds to set. Use a cake-decorator's icing
bag to pipe on cream spots, wings, or spindly legs.

or creamy blancmange!

Make up blancmange according to packet instructions. Pour
into molds, leave to set, then decorate to make your chosen
creepy-crawly. Sit on a bed of lime gelatin "grass", if desired.

crawly treats

Talk about farm

77

...look at farmyard books

baaa

78

...make animal noises

79

...make a toy farm

animals and...

moo

cluck
cluck

Sing animal rhymes!

hickory dickory dock

Hickory dickory dock,
the mouse ran up the clock.
The clock struck one,
the mouse ran down,
hickory dickory
dock.

81

itsy-bitsy spider

The itsy-bitsy spider climbed up the water spout,
down came the rain and washed the spider out.
Out came the sun and dried up all the rain,
And the itsy-bitsy spider climbed up the spout again.

82

two little dicky birds

Two little dicky birds sitting on a wall,
one named Peter, one named Paul.
Fly away Peter! Fly away Paul!
Come back Peter, come back Paul.

Go to the beach

83

...make
a splash

84

...build a
sandcastle

and...

85

...make footprints
in the sand

86

...dig a pool

87

...collect shells

88

"go down under"

Share your baby's perspective on things by getting down to her level and crawling around with her. Let her see how things look upside down by showing her how to peep through her own legs – she'll find it highly amusing.

89

"fly way up high"

Encourage your baby to get a new angle on the world by lifting her up high or onto your shoulders (mind her head!). This will give her a bird's-eye view of proceedings and will help to develop her sense of spatial awareness.

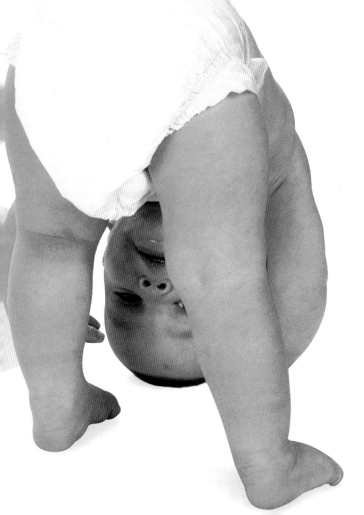

Do a workout

90

gently lift and rock

Once your baby is walking and his neck and back muscles are stronger, you can try new rough and tumble games, like this one. Tip your baby onto the soles of your feet, hold onto his arms, and rock him backward and forward in the air. When he's bigger, do the same thing, but support him on your shins.

touch your toes

This might be easier for
him than for you!

stretch your arms

Stand with feet apart and arms outstretched.
Lift your arms to the side to play "airplanes."

stretch your legs

Lie down on your back and swing one leg
over the other. See if your baby can do it, too.

94

play a game
of ball

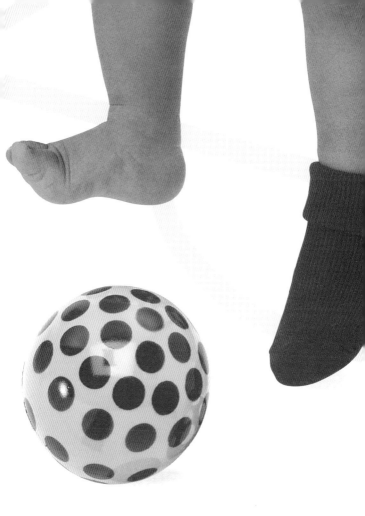

Make bathtime fun

95 ...bubbles

97 ...scooping and pouring

96 ...splashing and squirting

with...

go for a swim

Your baby will love the sensation of floating in a swimming pool from an early age – many young babies are more mobile in water than on dry land. You can take her to lessons or just regular sessions in the "baby" pool. She'll enjoy the swim and after, thanks to the exercise, she'll be relaxed and happy.

99

let him dry himself...

As part of your older baby's developing independence, make time for some DIY care! Start bathtime a little earlier and then let him dry himself and try to put on his pajamas, with as little help from you as possible. This is good fun for him and may well cut down on a lot of wriggling and complaining.

100

let him loose!

Young toddlers are exuberant about their bodies, and sometimes clothes can feel a little constricting. They much prefer to show off their birthday suits, loving the sensation of bare skin and running around with absolutely nothing on. So, after a bath, or when it's warm and sunny outside, let your child express himself with all his natural enthusiasm!

Fun-packed nursery rhymes

Babies enjoy rhymes from a very early age. Here are the words and actions of some you can try.

This little pig went to market

This little pig went to market,

[wiggle baby's big toe, then wiggle other toes in turn, ending with little toe]

This little pig stayed at home,

This little pig had roast beef,

This little pig had none,

And this little pig cried "Wee-wee-wee"

All the way home.

One, two, three, four, five…

One, two, three, four, five,

[count each finger on baby's left hand]

Once I caught a fish alive.

Six, seven, eight, nine, ten,

[count each finger on baby's right hand]

Then I let him go again.

Why did you let him go?

Because he bit my finger so!

Which finger did he bite?

This little finger on the right!

[wiggle baby's right-hand little finger]

Pat-a-cake

Pat-a-cake, pat-a-cake, baker's man,

[clap hands in rhythm]

Bake me a cake as fast as you can.

Pat it and prick it and mark it with B,

[pat and "prick" baby's hand, and trace a "B"]

And put it in the oven for Baby and me.

[pretend to slide cake into oven]

Here's a ball for baby

Here's a ball for baby,

Big and fat and round.

[cup your hands into ball shape]

Here is baby's hammer,

See how it can pound.

[hammer with your fist]

Here are baby's soldiers,

Standing in a row.

[point your fingers upward]

Here is baby's music,

Clapping, clapping so.

[clap your hands together]

Two little men in a flying saucer

Two little men in a flying saucer
Flew round the world one day.
[lift baby up and move in a circle]
They looked to the left and right a bit,
And couldn't bear the sight of it,
[cover baby's eyes with your hands]
And then they flew away.
[move baby's arms up and down]

Ride a cock horse

Ride a cock horse
To Banbury Cross,
To see a fine lady
Upon a white horse.
With rings on her fingers
And bells on her toes,
She shall have music
Wherever she goes.
[bob baby gently on knee throughout verse]

Round and round the garden

Round and round the garden,
[use forefinger to draw circle in baby's palm]
Like a teddy bear.
One step, two steps,
*[walk your fingers up your
baby's arm]*
Tickly under there.
[tickle under baby's arm]

Round and round the haystack,
[use forefinger to draw circle in baby's palm]
Went the little mouse.
One step, two steps,
*[walk fingers up your
baby's arm]*
In this little house.
[tickle under baby's arm]

Tommy Thumb

Tommy Thumb, Tommy Thumb,
Where are you?
Here I am, here I am,
[wiggle your baby's thumbs]
How do you do?

Do same with other fingers, naming them as:
Peter Pointer *(index),*
Toby Tall *(middle finger),*
Ruby Ring *(ring finger),*
Baby Small *(little finger)*

Fingers all, fingers all,
Where are you?
Here we are, here we are,
How do you do?
[wiggle all fingers]

Acknowledgments

Dorling Kindersley would like to thank the following:

Editorial and design

Dawn Bates and Caroline Greene for their editorial contributions, and Elly King, Bernhard Koppmeyer, Sally Smallwood and Dawn Young for their design assistance.

Photography

Andy Crawford, Jo Foord, Steve Gorton, Ruth Jenkinson, Dave King, David Murray, Ian O'Leary, Susanna Price, Tim Ridley, Jules Selmes and Steve Shott.

Picture credits

Front cover and swimming picture (idea 98) by kind permission of Mother & Baby Picture Library.

Nursery rhymes

The editors have made every effort to establish the identity of possible copyright holders for the nursery rhymes featured, but the investigations strongly suggest that the rhymes used are in the public domain.